CRYSTAL ALCHEMY

Let's Get Motivated

BY VIALET B RAYNE

TABLE OF CONTENTS

CRYSTALS

Azurite	**37**
Bumbee Bee Jasper	**39**
Carnelian	**43**
Kammerite	**45**
Orange Calcite	**51**
Sodalite	**53**

ESSENTIAL OILS

Cypress	**69**
Rosemary	**75**
Sweetgrass	**85**

HERBS

Blue Butterfly Pea	**97**
Orange	**105**
Peppermint	**117**

CRYSTAL GRIDS

Soaking Up Sunshine	**29**
Finding Clarity & Truth	**49**
Personal Power	**121**

WWW.DISCOVERYOURSPIRITUALGIFTS.COM | © 2023 VIALET B RAYNE

TABLE OF CONTENTS

MODULES

Move the Energy	**33**
Bumble Bee Jasper Ritual	**41**
Set the Course Ritual	**47**
Crystal Alchemist	**55**
Aromatic Blending	**63**
Removing Obstacles	**73**
Moon Cycles	**79**
Power of Words Ritual	**95**
Motivational Gift Set	**103**
Affirmations	**111**
Metatron's Cube	**123**
Genie Energy	**125**
Energy of May	**129**
Your Card Pull	**131**

ABOUT VIALET

Vialet is the magical creator of Discover Your Spiritual Gifts. She believes that we are meant to have abundant and joyful lives. Her mission is to provide individuals with the tools and resources to empower their lives. Vialet is a transformational healer, business coach, author, speaker, and teacher.

She is passionate about empowering other individuals to live better lives. Her students return over and over again to take her classes. Vialet provides a sacred space for learning and supports her students along their spiritual path. If you do not know where to start or what class to take first, schedule a time to meet with Vialet for direction. She loves assisting people on their spiritual journey.

Contact her at vialet@discoveryourspiritualgifts.com.

Vialet

Vialet B Rayne
Magical Creator of DYSG

CLASS GOALS

GOALS

My goals for this program are for YOU:

- To learn more about the Crystals, Herbs, and Essential Oils.
- To have fun connecting with these elements.
- To provide you with an opportunity to connect with others in our community.
- To integrate these tools into your daily life.

Soaking Up
Sunshine
Crystal Grid

- 5 Bumble Bee Jasper Towers
- 10 Orange Calcite Tumbled
- Bowl of Orange Calcite
- Selenite Bowl
- Yellow flowers

SOAKING UP SUNSHINE GRID

This grid brings the joy and energy of the sun into your life. It's masculine energy will motivate you to move forward and find your joy in this lifetime.

The Crystals

- **Bumble Bee Jasper:** Promotes happiness and joy. It teaches you how to celebrate each moment.
- **Orange Calcite:** Works with the lower energy centers to bring in creativity and the motivation to push through and forward. This crystal cleanses energy and uplift your spirits.

9

You can work with these crystals for creativity, motivation, and energy.

Setting Your Grid
1. Select your crystals and grid base.
2. Cleanse the crystals.
3. Set your intentions with the crystals.
4. Place the crystals on your grid.
5. Activate your grid.
6. Continue to work with your grid. Cleanse and re-activate the grid on a regular basis.

SECTION 1
CRYSTALS

MOVE THE ENERGY

Do you feel stuck or stagnant? Ever been stuck and didn't realize it right away?

Take a moment and think about your life.

You can be stuck emotionally, mentally, physically, or spiritually. Everything is energy and everything has frequency. Sometimes we struggle with moving forward or shifting the energies from their current state.

Situations that may lead to you feeling stuck or stagnant:
- Fear of making a change in your life
- Fear of failing in a situation or circumstance
- Fear of being rejected or taken seriously
- Fear of taking a risk
- Fear of taking responsibility or accountability in your life
- Fear of making the wrong choice or going in the wrong direction

Our fears can freeze us in place and prevent us from making changes or shifting directions.

13

#1. What Can You Do to Move Energy?

There are numerous ways to begin moving energy in the physical world. Here are a few suggestions:

Move furniture

Take time to think about your physical space at home and work. Where does the energy feel stuck in your rooms and space? Spend some time removing the clutter and deep cleaning the area. Start with a clean slate within the space. Donate items that no longer align with you and your lifestyle. Move the furniture around, while thinking about the flow of the energy in the space. What new energies can you bring in that align with you and the space? This can be color, style, decor, and fresh new perspectives.

Open the windows

On a warm day, open your windows and curtains and allow the fresh air to come into your space. Allow the fresh air to move out the stale and stagnant energy in your space.

Dancing

Play some uplifting music in your space and dance around the space. This exercise is not about being a professional dancer, It is about opening your heart and bringing joy into your space as you move the energy around your room(s).

Wind chimes

Hang a wind chime at the front door, in your space, or outside of your window. Wind chimes move the energy in the space. Find one that you love and hang it up!

Energetic sweep

The next time you sweep your space, take an energetic approach to sweeping. Set the intention that you are moving all the stuck energy around the space and out the door.

#2. What Should You Do?

Take some time in reflection. What are you doing or avoiding that will support your divine purpose? What needs to be released?

Take out a journal and begin setting the right intentions for yourself and your life. Begin focusing on where you need to be putting energy into in your life and start making changes that will assist you in moving forward.

_____
_____
_____
_____
_____

#3. What Do You Want to Do?

What are you spending your time doing? Where are you focusing your energy? Time is valuable. Think about where you are investing energy in your life. What do you want to be doing?

_____
_____
_____
_____
_____

CRYSTAL: AZURITE

*Intuitive Gifts * Clarity * Cleansing * Dissolves Blocks * Communication*

- **Elements:** Air
- **Chakras:** Third Eye & Crown
- **Planet:** Jupiter & Uranus
- **Colors:** Bright blue & light blue

 This crystal cannot be placed in water.

 This crystal cannot be placed in the sun

Key Elements

You can sometimes get tangled up in the cycles of worry and negativity. These cycles of energies will block you from moving forward. This crystal will dissolve the negative energies and emotions. It shines the light in the depths of your soul to bring clarity and purpose into your life.

17

This is an amazing crystal to assist you in standing in your power and speaking your truth. It will assist you in communication as it brings in your inner strength.

Azurite is an aura and chakra cleanser. It will remove and dissolve blocked energy in the physical. This crystal will open your third eye and enhance your psychic gifts.

In Ancient Egypt, this crystal was held in high reverence. It was used solely by the priests and priestesses in the temples. This crystal is believed to connect you with the lost city of Atlantis.

It has been called the Stone of Heaven. Azurite will build a strong connection to your guides and the higher realms. The beauty of this crystal will capture your attention.

CRYSTAL: BUMBLE BEE JASPER

*Change * Zest for Life * Confidence * Self-Esteem * Decision-making*

- **Elements:** Earth & Fire
- **Chakras:** Sacral & Solar Plexus
- **Planet:** Sun
- **Colors:** Yellow, black, & grey

 This crystal cannot be placed in water.

This crystal can be placed in the sun

Key Elements

Bumble Bee Jasper is formed from volcanic matter. It was discovered in 1990 on the Indonesian island, Java. It brings in strong earth energies. An unique stone that is hard to find.

This crystal attracts opportunities into your life. It assists in moving past the comfort zone and embracing change. Bumble Bee Jasper

19

attunes an individual in becoming more aware of golden opportunities. It enhances assertiveness, courage, and concentration.

It provides courage to move forward. This crystal clears blocks and obstacles preventing people from taking the steps needed to move forward. It gives an ego boost.

Bumble Bee Jasper energizes individuals. If the person is working on a major project or trying to manifest major changes in their lives, this is the perfect stone to assist them.

It supports quicker decision-making and thinking on your feet. This crystal is extremely useful when an individual needs to be creative and think outside of the box. It activates the imagination and enhances creativity.

a

BUMBLE BEE JASPER RITUAL

The crystal bumble bee jasper is not actually a jasper. It is a combination of volcano lava and sediment. It is gypsum, sulfur, and hematite. This crystal is a rare piece of magic, It is not easy to source, since the mine is inside an active Indonesian volcano. This crystal has not been found anywhere else.

This stone activates the Sacral and Solar Plexus Chakras. This crystal will amplify your creativity, build your confidence, and boost your momentum so that you can move forward.

What are your dreams and desires?

You can use Bumble Bee Jasper to get moving in life and create your dreams.

21

STEPS

- Pick up a **Bumble Bee Jasper** crystal.
- Get clear on your dreams and desires.
- Define one dream you would like to work towards. Be as specific as possible.
- Write down the details of your dream. Don't worry about how you will accomplish it.
- Hold your **Bumble Bee Jasper** in your right hand as you state your dream out loud.
- Connect with your crystal and ask for support and assistance in reaching your dream.
- Sit the crystal in a place that will remind of your goal.
- Hold a space of gratitude for what you will be manifesting into your life.

CRYSTAL: CARNELIAN

*Motivation * Courage * Confidence * Change * Choices*

- **Elements:** Fire
- **Chakras:** Root, Sacral, & Solar Plexus
- **Planet:** Sun & Mars
- **Colors:** Orange & Red

 This crystal can be placed in water.

 This crystal can be placed in the sun

Key Elements

This crystal brings in the energies of the sunset. It captivates with its bold energy and warmth. The Eqyptians called this stone, "the setting sun." It was traditionally worn to increase passion, love, and desire.

It is known as the **Stone of Motivation**. It holds the energies of endurance, leadership, and courage. Carnelian is the perfect stone

23

for creating harmony between mental focus and creativity to allow both the right and left brain to work together perfectly.

Carnelian is used by singers to boost their confidence and assist them in their power of true expression. It has been called the **Singer's Stone**.

This crystal is linked with Rose Quartz and it brings in the balance of sexual energy and the vibration of love. When you place both of the crystals at the heart chakra, you connect with your romantic and passionate side.

It is also a crystal for good luck and removes any thoughts of poverty consciousness. Many of the amulets and talismans worn by ancient warriors were made with carnelian to bring in courage, motivation, endurance, and leadership.

CRYSTAL: KAMMERERITE

*Emotional Balance * Motivation * Calming the Mind * Change*

- **Elements:** Water & Air
- **Chakras:** Throat, Third Eye, & Crown
- **Planet:** Neptune, Pluto, & Uranus
- **Colors:** Purple, violet, red, & black

 This crystal cannot be placed in water.

 This crystal can be placed in the sun

Key Elements

This is a rare crystal. It will assist the individual in bridging the energies between the spiritual and physical. One of the key elements is to provide a connection to your soul and allowing you to understand your purpose.

It is the perfect stone to calm the "Monkey Mind" and calm the overactive thoughts. This crystal can dissolve the negative patterns

25

of thinking. It will assist you in clearing the cycles that you can get stuck in.

This stones powerful energy is a stimulator for change. It will assist anyone that is ready to move forward into new things and new realities. Work with this crystal when you need clarity and direction in your life.

You will want to reach for this crystal when you are wanting more evolution and growth in your life. It is a gentle motivator for anyone that needs to be nudged in the right direction.

This crystal will support you in attracting more balanced and healthy relationships in your life. It teaches you the importance of balance with giving and taking from the relationship.

MODULE THREE
SET THE COURSE

SET THE COURSE RITUAL

When you have dreams and desires, it is easy to set goals. The challenge comes when we have to do the work to manifest it into this physical world. It takes determination and effort. This ritual will provide you with the determination you need to see things through to the finish line.

STEPS

- Sit in front of your altar and light a white candle.
- Cleanse the **Black Onyx** crystal. You may cleanse the Black Onyx crystal with white sage, Palo Santo, Sweetgrass, and/or Holy Water.
- Take a moment with the **Black Onyx** crystal. Set the intention for the crystal to support you in doing the work necessary to achieve your dreams and desires.
- Write down the descriptive or key words for what you are manifesting into your life.
- Fold the paper in half as many times as you can.
- Hold the folded paper and the **Black Onyx** crystal in your hands.
- Visualize the outcome and your celebration of accomplishment.

27

- State out loud, "I call forward all my guides, guardians, and master teachers to come and be with me. I allow only 100% Divine Love Aspect into this space. I ask for love, guidance, and support as I move toward my dreams and desires. Thank you. Thank you. Thank you."
- Allow yourself to be open and receptive to the guidance of the universe.
- Place the folded piece of paper and the **Black Onyx** crystal on your altar for 48 hours.
- At the end of 48 hours, burn the folded piece of paper safely in a burn resistant container.
- Place the **Black Onyx** crystal on your desk or within your workspace as a reminder of what you are manifesting.
- Hold a space of gratitude for all the energies that supported you in dissolving and removing any obstacles to your end goal with grace and ease.

Finding
Clarity & Truth
Crystal Grid

- Sodalite Point Center
- 7 Sodalite Tumbled
- 7 Clear Quartz Tumbled
- 13 Blue Kyanite Tumbled
- Dragonfly Silver Coins

FINDING CLARITY & TRUTH GRID

We sometimes get stuck because we are unclear on where to go next. This grid will assist you in becoming clear on your truth.

The Crystals

- **Sodalite**: This crystal will calm the mind. It encourages rational thought and brings in clarity.
- **Blue Kyanite**: The stone clears your fears and releases blocks in your throat chakra. It enhances self-expression and self-acceptance.

29

This grid will clear your mind so you may achieve clarity and purpose. You can work with these crystals to become clear on what is next for you and your life.

Setting Your Grid

1. Select your crystals and grid base.
2. Cleanse the crystals.
3. Set your intentions with the crystals.
4. Place the crystals on your grid.
5. Activate your grid.
6. Continue to work with your grid. Cleanse and re-activate the grid on a regular basis.

CRYSTAL: ORANGE CALCITE

*Creative * Energizing *Sexual Connection * Inspiration * Motivation*

- **Elements:** Fire
- **Chakras:** Sacral & Solar Plexus
- **Planet:** Sun
- **Colors:** Orange & yellow

 This crystal cannot be placed in water.

 This crystal cannot be placed in the sun

Key Elements

This is a strong, sacral crystal. It gets energies moving in the areas of creativity. It is an ideal stone for individuals looking for new ideas or innovative solutions. This crystal encourages you to see new perspectives and get going!

31

Orange Calcite brings in the energies of playfulness, lightheartedness, and confidence. It is a catalyst for inspiration and motivation in breaking old patterns.

This crystal assists in integrating the spiritual realm with your physical body. It is very helpful in balancing emotions and moods. Orange Calcite energizes and cleanses your lower chakras and energy fields.

It is the perfect cleansing stone to clear out stored negative energy and blocks that are preventing you from moving forward. It will clear out old emotional patterns and motivate you to take action.

This crystal brings in bursts of joy. It amplifies energies and brings in positivity. This is the perfect stone to carry in your pocket to get motivated.

32

CRYSTAL: SODALITE

*Spiritual Gifts * Creativity * Communicaton * Speaking * Calming*

- **Elements:** Air
- **Chakras:** Third Eye & Throat
- **Planet:** Venus
- **Colors:** Blue & white

 This crystal cannot be placed in water.

 This crystal can be placed in the sun

Key Elements

This crystal assists in the development of your spiritual gifts and enhancing your connection and intuition. The healing properies of the crystal supports teachers, writers, and students in integrating the deeper understandings of their studies and work. It also shines a spotlight on the idealism and truth within the subject.

33

Sodalite has strong metaphysical properties related to creativity. It stimulates new ideas. If you feel stuck and unable to find new ideas or thoughts, work with this stone. This crystal can trigger survival instincts to encourage balance of the mind and heart.

This is the perfect crystal for individuals that engage in public speaking. It aids in improving communication skills.

This crystal brings in positive thoughts and greater understanding. If you struggle with negative chatter, this is a great crystal to carry to bring in inspiration and confidence in who you are and what you are about.

It assists individuals that have panic attacks or anxiety. This crystal is calming and brings in emotional balance. Sodalite enhances self-esteem and self-acceptance.

CRYSTAL ALCHEMIST

In Sacred Alchemy, the students are moving through the seven stages of alchemy to gain the tools of transformation for their lives. The tools of alchemy provide transformation to shift your consciousness and put you on the path of spiritual ascension.

Stage #1: Calcination

This stage of alchemy will bring in transformation of the self through a series of alchemical processes where the individual's inner energies and consciousness change and expand on all levels. The inner alchemy works on unveiling the hidden aspects of oneself from the mysteries of the unconscious. This process of allowing the unbalanced energies within you to surface supports you in bringing you to back to your truth. The individual becomes aware of their ego and false truths.

Crystals for Calcination

- **Apache Tears**: Protection
- **Black Tourmaline**: Grounding
- **Desert Rose**: Dissolves Old Programs
- **Hematite**: Balances
- **Jet**: Activates the Kundalini

Source: www.art10zen.com

- **Pyrite:** Clearing Fears
- **Smoky Quartz:** Releasing Stress

Stage #2: Dissolution

This stage is dissolving all the false constructs of the mind by expanding your awareness. In this stage, the individual begins to question everything in their life, and they start to ask the big questions. This process will expand your spiritual gifts and begin to raise your consciousness to the next level.

Crystals for Dissolution

- **Astrophyllite**: Self-Mastery
- **Carnelian**: Regulates energy flow
- **Clear Quartz:** Cleanses
- **Green Aventurine**: Heals the body & mind
- **Lapis Lazuli:** Spiritual Development
- **Orange Calcite**: Balances sexual energies
- **Pink Mangano Calcite**: Opens the Heart
- **Prehnite**: Self-reflection

Stage #3: Separation

In this stage, the individual begins to separate their thoughts, feelings, and unconscious drives. They gain awareness from understanding and witnessing their habits, thoughts, feelings, and actions. Each of us is conditioned by our environment and influenced by the people in our lives. The individual begins to awaken to their own truth as they spark their own divine essence to come forward in their life.

Crystals for Separation

- **Ametrine**: Inspires Purpose
- **Chalcedony**: Dissolves Negativity
- **Citrine**: Clears Thoughts
- **Fluorite Purple**: Integraties Energies
- **Hematite**: Neutralizes Emotions
- **Kyanite Blue**: Releases Blocks
- **Lepidolite**: Clears Drama
- **Sunstone**: Brings in Opportunities
- **Tiger Eye Gold**: Brings Vitality
- **Yellow Calcite:** Balances Intellect

Stage #4: Conjunction

This is the stage where you begin to unite polarity consciousness and unify all the opposing energies for a higher state of being. The right and left side of the brain become more balanced and synchronized. It is the sacred union of the soul and spirit coming together as the conscious and unconscious mind begins to work together. Discernment becomes an important part of your life as you recognize the light and shadow aspects of your life.

Crystals for Conjunction

- **Chrysocolla**: Enhances Your Gifts
- **Dragons Blood Jasper**: Expands the Heart
- **Fluorite Green**: Protects Energy Fields
- **Kunzite Green**: Shields Aura
- **Pink Tourmaline:** Activates Heart Chakra

Stage #5: Fermentation

After you have completed the first four stages, you have begun to transform the old ego, personality, beliefs, and all the energies that were no longer serving you. In this stage, you start to magnetize the Spirit and connect to the higher dimensions of truth and wisdom. You will need to release the old self and rebirth your authentic self. This stage will bring in your divine passions as you integrate more with your Higher Self.

Crystals for Fermentation

- **Apatite Blue**: Cleanses Aura
- **Calcite Clear**: Releases Resistance
- **Celestite**: Opens Connection with Upper Dimensions
- **Danbrite**: Connects Upper Chakras
- **Merlinite:** Brings in Sacredness
- **Scolecite**: Expands Your Energy Field
- **Selenite:** Raises Consciousness

Stage #6: Distillation

In this stage, the individual begins to pull into the Crown Chakra the energies of the Divine. This enhances our gifts and connection. The individual will be forced to face any imbalances in their inflated ego and false programming. They begin to accept the shadow aspects of their personality, understanding the paradox of being human and Divine.

Crystals for Distillation

- **Astrophyllite:** Overcomes Distractions
- **Larimar:** Brings in Self-Acceptance

- **Lapis Lazuli:** Opens the Path of Enlightenment
- **Moldavite:** Raises Your Vibration
- **Spirit Quartz:** Stimulates Crown & Soul Star Chakras
- **Sugilite:** Protection from Negative Influences

Stage #7: Coagulation

This is the last stage of the process. The individual is mastering all of the dualities within their life and continues to raise their vibration. There is a spiritual light that permeates from them that can be seen throughout the universe. The Light Body is fully activated and bringing in a higher stage of consciousness in the physical.

Crystals for Coagulation
- **Diamond**: Expands Visionary Consciousness
- **Faden Quartz**: Accesses the Libraries
- **Lemurian Quartz**: Connects to Ancient Wisdom
- **Moldavite:** Transforms on All Levels

You can use these crystals to assist you in your transformation process. Where are you in your spiritual transformation? How is the alchemy showing up in your life?

SECTION 2

ESSENTIAL OILS

AROMATIC BLENDING

You may be drawn to blending your own essential oils by your own preferences and preferred aromas. It will be important to balance the top, middle, and base notes.

- **Top Notes:** An essential oil that is a top note evaporates quickly. This is the first scent that comes to the surface. These oils have a light, crisp, fresh, and airy aroma. Your citrus oils are top notes.

- **Middle Notes**: These essential oils have a soft, full-body scent, They have been called "heart notes", since they touch your heart. These scents can be difficult to identify in the blends, since these can include both top and base aromas.

- **Base Notes**: They will have intense, deep, earthy, and warm aromas. The base notes of the oils ground the blend. These will evaporate slowly.

The key to making a wonderful blend of essential oils is to balance the notes in the blend. Typically, the middle notes are about 75% of the blend, top notes make about 20% of the blend, and base notes are about 5%.

A popular blending ration is **3:5:2** which is 3 parts top note oils, 5 parts middle note oil and 2 parts base note oils, You should not need more than six different oils in your blend,

There is no right or wrong. You just need to start testing different blends with each other to find your favorites.

TOP/HEAD NOTES

These are the most volatile part of the blend. They are typically lighter notes like citrus notes (Bergamot & Lime), floral notes (Lavender & Rosemary), and green notes (Galbanum), When the individual smells the blend, these are the fragrances that have the pivotal role of being pleasing or unpleasing. They play a huge role in the initial reaction that someone has to a blend. These notes generally last 10-30 minutes before they evaporate.

Characteristics: Strong

MIDDLE/HEART NOTES

These are considered the soul of the blend, Their function is to retain some of the top notes while introducing some richer new scents to deepen your experience. The heart notes will last longer than the top notes. Since the blend is composed of 70% of these fragrances, they tend to last longer. These are the foundation of your blend. They will last 20-60 minutes.

Characteristics: Mellow

BASE/DRY DOWN NOTES

These are the foundation of the blend. They provide depth to the blend and will linger for a couple of hours. These are woodsy or mossy notes, They are stronger scents, These may last for days on clothing. This category will include baked and edible scents (vanilla, brown sugar, etc.), woodsy (sandalwood, patchouli, etc,), and musk.

Characteristics: Heavy

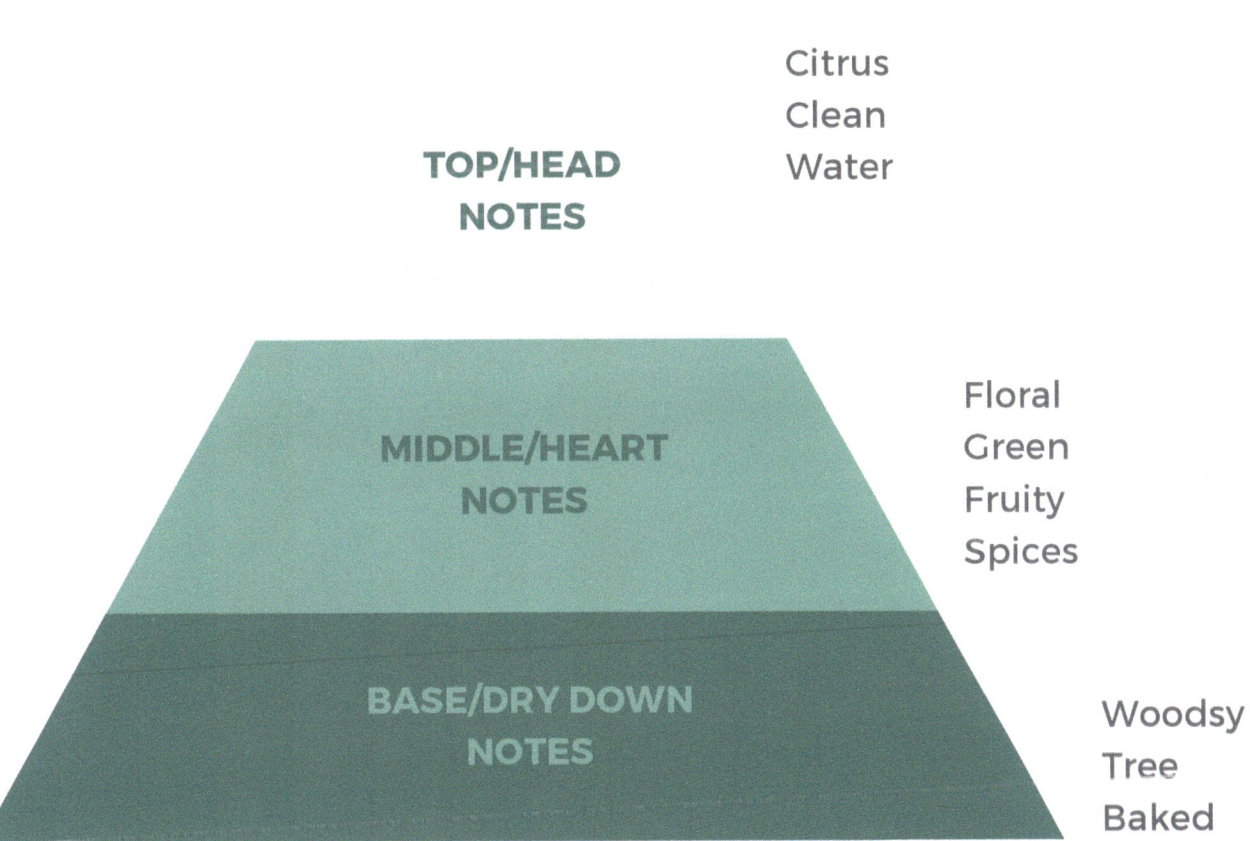

TOP/HEAD NOTES

Citrus
Clean
Water

MIDDLE/HEART NOTES

Floral
Green
Fruity
Spices

BASE/DRY DOWN NOTES

Woodsy
Tree
Baked

TOP NOTES

- Basil
- Bergmot
- Cinnamon
- Clary Sage
- Eucalyptus
- French Lavender
- Gardenia
- Grapefruit
- Honeysuckle
- Hyssop
- Lavender
- Lemon
- Lemongrass
- Lime
- Mandarin
- Myrtle
- Orange
- Peppermint
- Pine
- Rose Geranium
- Sage
- Spearmint
- Tangerine
- Tea Tree
- Thyme
- Verbena

MIDDLE NOTES

- Cardamon
- Chamomile
- Cinnamon
- Citronella
- Clary Sage
- Clove
- Cypress
- Fennel
- Geranium
- Heather
- Helichrysum
- Hibiscus
- Honeysuckle
- Hyssop
- Jasmine
- Juniper
- Lavender
- Marjoram
- Myrtle
- Nutmeg
- Pine
- Rose
- Rose Geranium
- Rosemary
- Thyme
- Violet
- Yarrow
- Ylang Ylang

BASE NOTES

- Angelica
- Cassia
- Cedarwood
- Cinnamon
- Frankincense
- Gardenia
- Ginger
- Helichrysum
- Jasmine
- Myrrh
- Oakmoss
- Patchouli
- Rose
- Sandalwood
- Spikenard
- Valeria
- Tobacco
- Valerian
- Vanilla
- Vetiver
- Ylang Ylang

FRAGRANCE PAPER STRIPS

An easy way to blend and test different essential oils is to use fragrance paper strips to test blends of fragrance. You can mark the strips for each of the essential oils.

EXAMPLE: 1 drop of Lemon, 2 drops of lavender and 2 drops of ylang ylang.

You can fan the strips with the drops of essential oil under your nose to test the blend of fragrances together.

47

Cypress
Essential Oil

- **Element:** Earth
- **Gender:** Feminine
- **Chakra:** Root & Third Eye
- **Planet:** Saturn
- **Astrology:** Aquarius. Cancer, & Capricorn
- **Deities:** Saturn, Hades, & Persephone

The Cypress tree has a calming effect that aids in healing and overcoming losses. The oil is comforting and healing for your heart. It can reconnect you with your inner child and bring more play, laughter, and fun into your life. It can bless your life with joy and happiness.

This oil is spiritually grounding and allows individuals to go with the flow and feel secure. The aroma energizes and gets you moving forward.

Spiritual benefits: acceptance, balance, calming, comfort, energizing, emotional balance, grief, grounding, growth, happiness, harmony, healing, hope, inner child, joy, laughter, play, security, stability, spiritual growth, spirituality, support, & transformation.

CYPRESS ESSENTIAL OIL USES

- **Apply, inhale, & diffuse**
- **Apply drops to:**
  - a dryer towel to freshen your laundry.
  - your shoes to reduce odor.
  - your household cleaning products.
  - your bath and shampoo products for freshness.
  - your skin toners to reduce oily skin.
- **Apply drops in a spray to:**
  - create a deodorizing furniture & room spray.
- **Apply diluted drops to your body for:**
  - opening breathing passages (apply to chest).
  - combating menopausal hot flashes.
  - opening your sacral and throat chakra.
- **Diffuse in your personal & workspace to bring in:**
  - calmness.
  - concentration.
  - emotional balance.
  - grounding.
  - protection.
- **Inhale from the bottle to:**
  - enhance breathing.
  - release blocks & obstacles.
- **Inhale from the bottle before meditating to:**
  - connect to your inner child.

BENEFITS

This essential oil assists with:

- Asthma
- Arthritis
- Carpal Tunnel
- Cold
- Cough
- Respiratory
- Varicose veins

MAIN PROPERTIES

- Anti-bacterial
- Anti-septic
- Anti-spasmodic

Disclaimer: I am a not medical professional and everything written here is from my own research. Don't take any advice given here over that of a certified medical professional. If you ingest any oils or herbs, always make sure that you're 100% certain that they're safe. If you're pregnant or giving to a child, always consult a doctor before ingesting any you aren't familiar with. The intention instruction are for personal entertainment purposes only.

OIL BLENDING

- **Aroma:** Balsamic & Woodsy
- **Perfume Note:** Base Note
- **Blends well with:** bay laurel, bergamot, cedarwood, clary sage, frankincense, lavender, lemon, lime, marjoram, orange, pine, rosemary, sandalwood, sage, & spikenard.

51

Diffuser: Italian Spring

- 3 drops of Cypress
- 3 drops of Lemon
- 3 drops of Bergamot

Diffuser: Walk in the Woods

- 3 drops of White Fir
- 3 drops of Cypress
- 2 drops of Frankincense
- 1 drop of Clove
- 1 drop of Peppermint

Rollerball Blend: Reduce Varicose/Spider Veins

- 5 ml rollerball bottle
- 3 drops of Cypress oil
- 2 drops of Lavender
- 1 drop of Citrus Fresh
- Fractionated Coconut oil

REMOVING OBSTACLES

Sometimes we encounter obstacles in our lives. These obstacles may seem impossible to overcome. You may need a new perspective, or you may need to dissolve the obstacle. This ritual will assist you in banishing the obstacle.

STEPS:

- Sit in front of your altar and light a white candle.
- Cleanse the **Bloodstone** crystal. You may cleanse the Bloodstone crystal with white sage, Palo Santo, Sweetgrass, and/or Holy Water.
- Take a moment with the **Bloodstone** crystal. Set the intention for the crystal to support you in removing the obstacle(s).
- Write down the descriptive or key word(s) of the obstacle(s) on a piece of paper.
- Fold the paper in half as many times as you can.
- Tie the paper with a string and/or ribbon to the **Bloodstone** crystal.
- Visualize the current situation with the obstacle(s).
- Set your intention that you will remove the obstacle(s) with grace and ease.

- Visualize the obstacle being dissolved and disappearing from your vision.
- Leave the **Bloodstone** crystal tied to the paper on your altar for 24 hours.
- After 24 hours, cut the string and/or ribbon, remove the paper, and burn the paper safely.
- Hold the crystal while visualizing success in all areas.
- Hold a space of gratitude for all the energies that supported you in dissolving and removing the obstacle with grace and ease.

SOURCE: *Crystal Magic: Mineral Wisdom for Pagans & Wiccans* by Sandra Kynes

Rosemary
Essential Oil

- **Element:** Fire & Air
- **Gender:** Masculine
- **Chakra:** Throat, Third Eye, & Crown
- **Planet:** Sun
- **Astrology:** Leo
- **Deities:** Fairies, Hebe, Aphrodite, & the Virgin Mary

This oil brings in mental clarity and focus. It helps with overcoming feelings of exhaustion and fatigue. Rosemary is great for relieving stress and reducing anxiety.

Historical: Rosemary was associated with love and friendship in Medieval times. In Shakespeare's time, it was believed to improve memory.

Spiritual benefits: accuracy, alertness, clarity, cleansing, concentration, emotional balance, fertility, focus, healing, luck, mental clarity, protection, purification, purpose, tranquility, & uplifting

ROSEMARY ESSENTIAL OIL USES

- **Apply, inhale, & diffuse**
- **Apply drops to:**
  - your candle intention for protection.
  - your candle intention to clear blocks.
  - your household cleaning products for energetic cleansing.
  - your bath products to bring in happiness.
  - your sacred bath for spiritual cleansing.
- **Apply drops in a spray to:**
  - create a bug-repellant.
- **Apply diluted drops to your body for:**
  - pain relief.
  - relieve a headache. Apply to temples.
- **Diffuse in your personal & workspace to bring in:**
  - cleansing energies within the space.
  - enhance concentration.
  - improve memory.
  - uplift your mood.
- **Inhale from the bottle to:**
  - boost your focus in the afternoon.
  - energize after a meal.
  - release anxious energy.
- **Inhale from the bottle before meditating to:**
  - bring in focus.

BENEFITS

This essential oil assists with:

- Anxiety
- Arthritis
- Bad breath
- Blood Circulation
- Cough
- Dandruff
- Hair growth
- Headaches
- Memory
- Pain
- Respiratory
- Stress

MAIN PROPERTIES

- Anti-bacterial
- Anti-fungal
- Anti-oxidant
- Anti-septic
- Anti-viral

Disclaimer: I am a not medical professional and everything written here is from my own research. Don't take any advice given here over that of a certified medical professional. If you ingest any oils or herbs, always make sure that you're 100% certain that they're safe. If you're pregnant or giving to a child, always consult a doctor before ingesting any you aren't familiar with. The intention instruction are for personal entertainment purposes only.

OIL BLENDING

- **Aroma:** Herbal
- **Perfume Note:** Middle Note
- **Blends well with:** basil, cedarwood, frankincense, geranium, ginger, grapefruit, lemongrass, lime, orange, peppermint & tangerine

Take a Breath Rollerball Blend

- 4 drops Rosemary oil
- 4 drops Eucalyptus oil
- 2 drops Peppermint oil
- Carrier oil
- Rollerball bottle

Diffuser: Bring in Focus

- 2 drops of Rosemary oil
- 2 drops of Lavender
- 3 drops of Bergamot

Zesty Bath Salts

- 1 cup Dead Sea Salt
- 1 cup Epsom Salt
- 1 cup Baking Soda
- ½ cup Power Milk
- 6 drops of Rosemary oil
- 6 drops of Lemon oil

Spread your salt mixture on a cookie sheet to dry. Takes 48 hours to dry.

MOON CYCLES

The phases of the Moon are caused by the relative positions of the Sun, Moon, and Earth. The moon does not produce visible light on its own. You can only see the parts of the moon that are lit up by other objects in the sky. The moon is lit by distant stars and the reflection of the light from the Earth. The main source of light is from the Sun.

The moon goes through multiple stages of partial illumination during the different phases of the moon. Each of the phases of the moon is a position in the full 29.5 day cycle. There are eight phases of the moon including:

- New Moon
- Waxing Crescent Moon
- First Quarter Moon
- Waxing Gibbous Moon
- Full Moon
- Waning Gibbous Moon
- Last Quarter Moon
- Waning Crescent Moon

59

WAXING & WANING

When you understand the difference between the moon growing or shrinking, you will know the difference between a waxing or waning moon.

WAXING MOON

A waxing moon is when the moon is getting closer to being full size. This is the phase of the moon developing to a full moon. An easier way to remember is a waxing moon is "maxing" out the size.

The waxing moon occurs after the new moon appears and continues to become larger moving towards the full moon. During this phase of the cycle, the right side of the moon is illuminated and it resembles the letter D.

WANING MOON

A waning moon is when the moon is moving past the full moon. It concludes in complete darkness. The left side of the moon is illuminated and it looks like the letter C.

NEW MOON

The new moon is the start of a new lunar cycle. It is the invisible phase of the Moon, The moon is the darkest and it will sometimes be called the dark moon. The illuminated side faces the Sun and the night side faces the Earth.

CRESCENT MOON

The moon is moving towards a state of fullness. This phase of the moon is bringing in change and new opportunities.

GIBBOUS MOON

The moon appears more than half lit. It is the last phase before the moon has reaches fullness. This is time for expansion and growth. It is the time to chase after your wildest dreams and desires.

FULL MOON

The full moon illuminates a time of heighten emotions and possibilities. This moon offers you the opportunity to sit in the fullness of your life.

SPIRITUAL PRACTICES

What are some of the spiritual practices that you can do during the different cycles of the moon? For the individuals that love the cycles of the moon, the energies can support you and your spiritual practices.

NEW MOON - NEW BEGINNINGS

It symbolizes new beginnings. This is the perfect time to start a new projects, new rituals, new intentions, etc.

- Light a candle and acknowledge the new things in your life.
- Take action by setting clear and defined intention.
- Clarify your goals and visualize the outcome.
- Start somethings new (start a class).
- Try something new (check out a new restaurant).

61

- Reset your altar and focus on new beginnings.
- Set some new rituals for your spiritual practices.
- Journal about new ideas, new goals, and new intentions.
- Accept invitations to meet new people or to experience new things.

WAXING MOON - TAKE ACTION

It symbolizes the growth of the seeds that were planted during the new moon. This is the time to take action to move your intention forward.

- Light a candle and reflect on the intentions set during the new moon.
- Create an action item list for you to do to support the intentions that have been set.
- Schedule time to get in motion with committing to your action list.
- Become mindful of your decisions and create alignment with your intentions.

EXAMPLE: You have set an intention in the New Moon cycle to make healthier food choices. The action items in the waxing moon may be:

- Clean out your pantry and refrigerator eliminating unhealthy choices.
- Find new healthy recipes to try.
- Prep food that aligns with your schedule.

FULL MOON - COMPLETION

It symbolizes the end of a cycle. This is an opportunity for transformation and change. Everything is in full illumination, so there is light being shined on all aspects of your life. This is the time to ask the question: What is working? What needs to be released?

- Light a candle and reflect on your life.
- Make a list of the accomplishments and good things in your life.
- Hold a space of gratitude for your life.
- Conduct a burning ceremony to release/dissolve things in your life.
- Review your to-do list and schedule. Remove the things that do not bring you joy and happiness.

WANING MOON - SURRENDER

It symbolizes the decreasing light of the moon. This cycle reminds us to surrender and renew our energies. This is the time to pause and recharge your energies.

- Make time for self-care for yourself.
- Declutter your space and work on a deep cleaning project.
- Take a day to recharge by getting more rest, saying no to someone or something that drains you, or make time to be alone.
- Allow the universe and your guides to take the wheel of something that means a lot to you.

If you love working with the Moon energies, check our my monthly Moon Ceremonies. These bring in a mixture of moon energy, magick, ritual, and ceremony.

Find out more at: https://discoveryourspiritualgifts.com/moon-ceremony

Sweetgrass
Essential Oil

- **Element:** Water
- **Gender:** Feminine
- **Chakra:** Root
- **Planet:** Venus
- **Astrology:** Taurus
- **Deities:** Native American Indian

Sweetgrass is considered a holy herb by many Native American tribes. It has a unique vanilla aroma when it is burned. This herb is believed to represent the hair of Mother Earth. It attracts positive energies when it is burned. This herb was used as a sacred medicine.

In Northern Europe, they would lay sweetgrass in front of the church on Saint's Day. The sweet aroma would be released as individuals walked on it.

Sweetgrass was stuffed into pillows and mattresses with the hopes of having sweet dreams.

Spiritual benefits: ancestors, calming, cleansing, dreams, harmony, hope, love, luck, new beginnings, peace, protection, purity, purification, rebirth, relaxation, strength, & spiritual attraction

SWEETGRASS ESSENTIAL OIL USES

- **Apply, inhale, & diffuse**
- **Apply drops to tea or water to:**
  - clear congestion & nasal passages.
  - relieve a cold or cough.
  - treat sore throats.
- **Apply drops to:**
  - your bath & beauty products to sweeten your day.
  - your massage oil to shift your mood.
  - your sacred bath for relaxation.
  - your candle intentions to bring in peace.
  - your eye wash solution to heal windburn.
- **Apply drops in a spray to:**
  - cleanse your auric field.
- **Diffuse in your personal & workspace to bring in:**
  - attract positive spirits.
  - calmness.
  - freshness.
  - home blessings.
  - protection.
  - relaxation.
- **Inhale from the bottle to:**
  - bring in relaxation.
  - enhance calmness.
- **Inhale from the bottle before meditating to:**
  - calm anxiety.

66

BENEFITS

This essential oil assists with:

- Colds
- Cough
- Eye infections
- Reproductive health

MAIN PROPERTIES

- N/A

Disclaimer: I am a not medical professional and everything written here is from my own research. Don't take any advice given here over that of a certified medical professional. If you ingest any oils or herbs, always make sure that you're 100% certain that they're safe. If you're pregnant or giving to a child, always consult a doctor before ingesting any you aren't familiar with. The intention instruction are for personal entertainment purposes only.

OIL BLENDING

- **Aroma:** Earthy & Herbal
- **Perfume Note:** Top Note
- **Blends well with:** bergamot, frankincense, lavender, pine, sandalwood, spikenard, white sage, & ylang ylang

SECTION 3

HERBS

POWER OF WORDS RITUAL

The two most powerful words are "I AM" and this includes the power of both positive and negative statements you are making in your life.

How often have you made these statements in your mind or out loud?

- I AM stupid.
- I AM unlovable.
- I AM a failure.
- I AM poor.
- I AM unlucky.

You may have collected these beliefs in your childhood. Someone in your family may have told you that you would not be able to do something and you took it as your truth.

When you think or say something as a negative statement, it takes seconds for that statement to be sent out into the universe to be manifested in our reality. It is important that you are consciously aware of what we are saying to ourselves and others.

71

When you make a negative statement, you need to have a ritual that will cancel, dissolve, and/or release the statement. Here is a ritual that I use in my life every day:

I AM exhausted and overwhelmed.

Cancel, cancel, cancel

Delete, delete, delete

Erase, erase, erase

I AM energized and focused.

KEY ELEMENTS

- The universe does not recognize NOT. I AM NOT tired. The universe will read it as I AM tired.
- It take seconds to manifest your thoughts and words. You must become more aware of these in your daily life.
- The power of three will amplify your ritual and shift the energies of your statement.

BUTTERFLY PEA

This plant is native to Asia and is well-established in Australia. There is a white variety of this plant, but the blue variety is the most popular. In India, this plant is known as the Aprarjita flower. It is named after the Hindu goddess. It is said that Shiva and Vishnu also loved these flowers.

When the herb is used in tea, it is visually appealing and has a mild earthy flavor. It is commonly used as a natural food coloring agent for various dishes and desserts.

This herb has the transformational effects of butterfly energy. It will support you in moving through change with grace.

Element: Water
Gender: Feminine
Chakra: Third Eye
Planet: Venus
Astrology: Unknown

Tarot Energies
- II High Priestess
- III Empress
- VI Lovers
- IX Hermit
- XVII The Star

Month Energies
- January: New Beginnings
- February: Self Love
- June: Growth
- September: Reflection
- November: Service & Gratitude

ENERGIES
awareness, enlightenment, expansion, fertility, gratitude, growth, healing, inner strength, love, peace, perseverance, protection, self-love, serenity, sexuality, spirituality, success, transformation, & tranquility

MAGICAL USES
- Charm bags
- Dream sachets
- Incense mixture
- Intention bottles
- Tea blends

SUGGESTIONS:
- **You can add to your tea recipes to:**
  - bring in change and transformation.
  - enhance your moon ceremony.
  - promote mental clarity.
  - release limiting beliefs.
  - relieve anxiety.
  - see the beauty in the world.
- **Add to your magic and rituals to:**
  - your candle intention for support with change.
  - your candle intention to attract love.
  - your dream sachet for peaceful sleep.
  - your mojo bag for beauty and love.
  - your sacred bath to bring in self-love.

- **You can place it on your altar and/or space for:**
  - alignment with the moon cycles.
  - clarity to your meditation work.
  - expanded awareness in your spiritual journey.
  - reminding you to listen to your inner guidance.

HEALTH BENEFITS

This essential oil assists with:

- Anxiety
- Asthma
- Blood sugar
- Cholesterol
- Depression
- Digestion
- Eyesight
- Hair growth
- Immunity
- Memory
- Pain
- Respiratory
- Seizures
- Swelling

MAIN PROPERTIES

- Anti-inflammatory
- Anti-oxidants

Disclaimer: I am a not medical professional and everything written here is from my own research. Don't take any advice given here over that of a certified medical professional. If you ingest any oils or herbs, always make sure that you're 100% certain that they're safe. If you're pregnant or giving to a child, always consult a doctor before ingesting any you aren't familiar with. The intention instruction are for personal entertainment purposes only.

BUTTERFLY PEA TEA BLEND

This herb is a great addition to your tea blends. Use organic herbs and create your blend. You can blend to your own personal taste. Feel free to add a touch of honey for sweetness.

Best herbs to blend with **BUTTERFLY PEA:**

- Chamomile
- Cornflower
- Ginger
- Heather
- Hibiscus
- Jasmine
- Lavender
- Lemon
- Lemongrass
- Licorice
- Peppermint
- Rosehips
- Spearmint
- Vanilla

BLEND TO YOUR TASTE & HEALTH NEEDS

77

MOTIVATION GIFT SET

You can provide someone with a crystal gift set when they need some motivation to move forward. Often, it is about taking one step at a time. When you are overwhelmed or lost, these crystals can provide you with the motivation to start taking steps forward.

- **Carnelian:** This crystal promotes positive change and life choices. It motivates the individual towards success. Carnelian gives the individual courage and dissolves doubts.
- **Citrine**: This crystal activates creativity and encourages self-expression. It enhances the individual's concentration and focus, so they can move forward. Citrine releases fears, doubts, and depression.
- **Lapis Lazuli**: This crystal encourages self-awareness and reveals the individual's inner truth. It stimulates objectivity and clarity. Lapis Lazuli inspires confidence and integrity.
- **Pyrite**: This crystal provides a protective shield when you need it the most. It blocks negative energy and promotes emotional well-being. Pyrite brings in good luck and prosperity.

- **Red Jasper**: This crystal is comforting, and it will give you strength to set your foundation and move forward. It assists you in taking on new pursuits. Red Jasper will support your efforts to take action towards a more stable environment.
- **Red Tiger's Eye:** This crystal brings in confidence and self-esteem. It motivates the individual to move forward in making choices and taking action. Red Tiger's Eye inspires and uplifts in the midst of adversity.

ORANGE

Orange powder and peel bring in joy and happiness. You can place oranges on your altar to bring in luck, money, and prosperity.

Orange blossoms can be used with lust and love intentions. Couples may want to add oranges to their tea to ensure martial bliss.

Citrus fruits such as oranges, lemons, limes, grapefruits, and tangerines have powerful, health-promoting properties.

Oranges bring happiness and joy into your life. They bring in money, prosperity, and success. Orange will inspire and uplift you. This is a great herb for aligning you with your divine purpose. Oranges in your bath attract love and companionship.

Element: Earth & Fire
Gender: Masculine
Chakra: Heart, Sacral, & Solar Plexus
Planet: Sun

Astrology
- Leo
- Sagittarius
- Virgo

Tarot Energies
- III Empress
- VI Lovers
- XIX Sun
- XXI World

Month Energies
- March: Connections
- April: Confidence
- May: Motivation
- July: Family/Celebrations
- October: Magic
- November: Service & Gratitude

ENERGIES
abundance, attraction, awakening, balance, beauty, calming, career, cheerfulness, confidence, creativity, energizing, fertility, friendship, happiness, harmony, healing, joy, laughter, love, luck, marriage, money, new beginnings, peace, play, positivity, prosperity, renewal, sovereignty, success, & uplifting

MAGICAL USES

- Charm bags
- Dream sachets
- Incense mixture
- Intention bottles
- Tea blends

SUGGESTIONS:

- **You can add to your tea recipes to:**
  - add confidence in your day.
  - bring in happiness & joy.
  - enhance your creativity.
- **You can add to your magic and rituals to:**
  - attract the right people in your life.
  - bring in prosperity.
  - household magic by hanging dried oranges in the windows.
  - bring in happiness and joy.
- **You can place it on your altar and/or space to add:**
  - luck & good fortune to your life.
  - happiness In your relationships.
  - the flow of prosperity.

Drink a large glass of orange juice before making a big decision.

HEALTH BENEFITS

This essential oil assists with:

- Anemia
- Anxiety
- Appetite-suppressant
- Asthma
- Cholesterol
- Digestive
- Fevers
- Headache
- Insomnia
- Kidney

MAIN PROPERTIES

- Anti-bacterial
- Anti-fungal
- Anti-inflammatory
- Anti-oxidant

Disclaimer: I am a not medical professional and everything written here is from my own research. Don't take any advice given here over that of a certified medical professional. If you ingest any oils or herbs, always make sure that you're 100% certain that they're safe. If you're pregnant or giving to a child, always consult a doctor before ingesting any you aren't familiar with. The intention instruction are for personal entertainment purposes only.

ORANGE TEA BLEND

This herb is a great addition to your tea blends. Use organic herbs and create your blend. You can blend to your own personal taste. Feel free to add a touch of honey for sweetness.

Best herbs to blend with **ORANGE:**

- Astragalus
- Cardamon
- Cinnamon
- Clove
- Ginger
- Hibiscus
- Lavender
- Lemon
- Lemongrass
- Peppermint
- Raspberry Leaf
- Rooibos
- Rose

BLEND TO YOUR TASTE & HEALTH NEEDS

- Rosehips
- Rosemary
- Safflower
- Sage
- Spearmint
- Tangerine
- Thyme

84

MOTIVATIONAL BATH

Bath Ritual

Take time to detox your emotional, mental, and physical bodies of negative and imbalanced energies. It will remove toxins and provide a restful night's sleep.

Take time to light a candle and to set sacred space for a bath. NOTE: If you use a disposable tea bag for your herbs, it will make cleaning the tub easier.

Ingredients
- 1 cup Sea salt
- 1 cup Epsom salt
- ½ cup Baking soda
- ½ cup Dried milk

- 4 green tea bags
- 5-7 drops of grapefruit essential oil
- 2 Citrine tumbled stones
- 3 grapefruit, sliced

Ritual

1. Hold the intention.
2. Light a candle.
3. Run a bath at your favorite temperature.
4. Add the salts, baking soda, dried milk, green tea bags with slices of grapefruit, and grapefruit essential oils.
5. Step into the bath.
6. Hold the citrine crystals in your hands.
7. Focus on your intention.
8. Allow yourself to listen and receive.

MODULE TEN

AFFIRMATIONS

Affirmations are phrases that repeat to ourselves or out loud to shift negative thoughts or statements that we are repeating in our lives. Some individuals will journal, write the phrase over and over again, or post it in a visible space to be seen throughout the day.

They can be created as a series of statements or a single phrase. The affirmation should always be written or stated in a positive manner. The words that are used are very important.

Think about these:
- I may
- I can
- I will
- I have
- I am

How do these vary in energies and understanding? Which ones would you think hold the power for change?

THOUGHT PATTERNS

What is the real purpose of using affirmations in our lives? They are used to reprogram the thoughts that are running in our subconscious. These thoughts and statements have been created based on our experiences.

- The statements that you have made in your mind about yourself, others, or situations. Example: I hate my job.
- The statements that have been told to you. Example: Men are bad. You will never be successful.
- The beliefs that you have about the outcomes that have occurred in your life. Example: If I go snow skiing, I will break my leg like Jason did.

All of these are planting seeds within your subconscious that becomes the mental chatter that is cycling in your mind. Your mind is very powerful. It is part of the mechanism that is creating your reality. This mental chatter can be compared to the back seat driver that is telling you how to drive and where to go. It can be difficult to ignore the individuals behind you giving you input from the back seat.

Some of these seeds may have been planted at a very young age and you don't remember the conversation or situation, but you have taken it as your truth.

How can you begin to shift these?

88

AWARENESS

The first step is to become consciously aware of the thoughts that are happening in your mind. When you notice that you are having a negative thought or reaction, you need to ask yourself some questions:

1. What is my truth?
2. Why do I believe this?
3. What is the emotion that is attached to this?
4. When did I first believe this?

Take the time to process the thoughts and emotions that are attached to these thoughts. It will be important to keep asking yourself deeper and deeper questions until you find the root of the seed that was planted.

After you have done some internal work on understanding how the thoughts have been created, you can begin to shift these energies. The next time the thought occurs, you should state in your mind: CANCEL, CANCEL, CANCEL. This will begin the process of healing to clear the thought in the subconscious. The next step will be to replace the thought with a positive thought.

EXAMPLE

- You hear this thought in your mind, "You cannot do that. You will fail."
- You will immediately state, "Cancel, Cancel, Cancel." It is important that you state three times.

- Take some deep clearing breaths.
- You state in your mind, "I have all the tools that I need to be successful. I have all the tools that I need to be successful. I have all the tools that I need to be successful." You will replace the thoughts with a positive statement by stating it three times.

You will want to use powerful statements of affirmations. It can also be used as a visual until you have re-programmed your mind with new phrases. You can create a visual to display in your space.

BLOCKS

What will block your affirmation work? There are individuals that will not effectively work with affirmations. You need to understand some of the mechanics of universal laws and energies.

#1. Heart and Mind Connection

You are manifesting the things in your life that are connecting the thoughts and emotions. Your center is your power energy center. If you are using affirmations around you being beautiful, but emotionally you do not believe what you saying. The affirmation will not work. You must be able to emotionally connect with what you are saying.

#2. Fake until you make it

There is something to be said about the saying, "You need to fake it til you make it." When you achieve it, what will your emotional reaction be? You will need to connect with those emotions and dissolve any doubts that you hold.

#3. *Visualize the outcome*
Take the time to day dream and visualize the affirmation becoming reality.

Ask yourself questions
- How will others react?
- What will be your reaction?
- What will happen next?
- How does this impact you?

Pay attention to any hidden or deep fears that you may have about it manifesting in your life. You will need to do some healing work on some of those deep seeds. After you have uncovered any blocks, began to day dream and visualize it manifesting with grace and ease.

DECLARATIONS
Some of the most powerful affirmations are the ones that are creating from a space of declaration. The individual is solid in their view of the affirmation.

They are not wishing, They are not asking. They are not dreaming. They are making a declaration to attract or manifest in their life. When was the last time that you set a goal and you were determined to achieve it? Set yourself up for success and go for your dreams!

91

PEPPERMINT

Peppermint is a natural hybrid of spearmint and water mint. It is the most popular of the mint family. In Greek mythology, Menthe was turned into a peppermint plant when Proserpine (Persephone), in a jealous rage, found out that Pluto (Hades) was in love with her. Even earlier, Assyrians used peppermint as an offering to their fire god.

According to Scott Cunningham, peppermint increases the vibrations of a place and expels negative energy. You can add it to sachets, oils, baths, or teas. If the plant is kept in the home it clears and purifies.

Element: Air
Gender: Masculine
Chakra: Heart, Throat, & Crown
Planet: Venus & Pluto

Astrology
- Cancer
- Libra
- Scorpio

Tarot Energies
- III Empress
- IV Emperor
- VII Chariot
- X Wheel of Fortune

Month Energies
- May: Motivation
- June: Growth
- September: Reflection
- November: Service & Gratitude

93

MAGICAL USES

- Charm bags
- Dream sachets
- Incense mixture
- Intention bottles
- Tea blends

SUGGESTIONS:

- **You can add to your tea recipes to:**
  - bring in focus & concentration.
  - cleanse the energies in the physical.
  - get in motion & move forward.
- **You can burn to bring in:**
  - cleansing.
  - concentration.
  - purification.
- **You can add to your magic and rituals to:**
  - your sacred bath for decision-making.
  - your intention jar for clarity.
  - your money mojo bag for money flow.
  - your sachet to support change & moment.

- **You can place it on your altar and/or space to:**
  - bring in financial flow & abundance.

HEALTH BENEFITS

This essential oil assists with:

- Fertility
- Hypertension
- Menopause
- Respiratory

MAIN PROPERTIES
- **Muscle Relaxant**
- **Anti-bacterial**
- **Digestion Support**

Disclaimer: I am a not medical professional and everything written here is from my own research. Don't take any advice given here over that of a certified medical professional. If you ingest any oils or herbs, always make sure that you're 100% certain that they're safe. If you're pregnant or giving to a child, always consult a doctor before ingesting any you aren't familiar with. The intention instruction are for personal entertainment purposes only.

PEPPERMINT TEA BLEND

This herb is a great addition to your tea blends. Use organic herbs and create your blend. You can blend to your own personal taste. Feel free to add a touch of honey for sweetness.

Best herbs to blend with **PEPPERMINT:**

- Cassia
- Chamomile
- Cinnamon
- Clove
- Fennel
- Ginger
- Holy Basil
- Hibiscus
- Lavender
- Lemon
- Lemongrass
- Linden Flower
- Marshmallow Root
- Nettle
- Orange
- Raspberry Leaf
- Red Clover
- Rosehips
- Rosemary
- Spearmint
- St. John's Wort
- Vanilla

BLEND TO YOUR TASTE & HEALTH NEEDS

96

Lighting Your
PERSONAL POWER
Crystal Grid

- Bumble Bee Jasper Heart
- 7 Citrine Tumbled
- 6 Honey Calcite Tumbled
- Sunflower Coins
- Flowers

LIGHTING YOUR PERSONAL POWER GRID

You may just need a boost in the right direction. This grid will support you as it pushes you forward in your daily activities.

The Crystals:

- **Bumble Bee:** You can connect to the joy in this crystal. It will motivate you to get going.
- **Citrine:** This crystal will get you focused on the finish line. It enhances your energy to move forward.
- **Honey Calcite**: It teaches you how to use your personal power for the right things. This crystal will require that you take responsibility.

97

You can hold or carry these crystals when you are ready to step into your personal power.

Setting Your Grid

1. Select your crystals and grid base.
2. Cleanse the crystals.
3. Set your intentions with the crystals.
4. Place the crystals on your grid.
5. Activate your grid.
6. Continue to work with your grid. Cleanse and re-activate the grid on a regular basis.

METATRON'S CUBE

This sacred symbol starts with the Fruit of Life shape. It connects all the 13 circles with lines. Metatron's cube contains all five of the Platonic Solids hidden within the symbol. This symbol is named after Archangel Metatron. Metatron watches over the flow of the energy of creation in the universe.

This symbol brings in the energies of balance, harmony, creation, protection, and healing. You may use it for healing, for balance and harmony, protection for you and your space, and creation for manifesting your dreams.

Uses

You may use a wooden, metal, or cloth Metatron's Cube to bring in the energies you need:

- **PROTECTION**: Place at the front door, under your flooring, under your bed, etc.
- **HEALING**: Place under your bed, massage table, client chairs, etc.
- **BALANCE**: Place on a altar, in a crystal grid, under your bed, etc.

Get creative and use Metatron's cube in your space and life.

GENIE ENERGY

The word genie derives from the Arabic word jinni, which means spiritual being or spirit. According to Islamic mythology, genies were created from smokeless fire. They had free will and the ability to shapeshift. The term genie was first introduced in the 18th-century Arabian Nights tales. These spiritual beings were magical and granted wishes to humans.

These spiritual beings are not exclusive to Islamic mythology. They can be found in various cultures and stories around the world. One of the most popular fictional characters is the magical genie in the Disney movie, Aladdin. The genie appeared from the magical lantern in a puff of smoke. He captured our hearts with his personality and heart. Robin Williams and Will Smith allowed us to personally connect with these magical beings.

Why was the genie blue in Aladdin?

According to Richard Plum, an ornithologist from Yale University, how the individual sees the color blue is related to how light works. In his perspective, the genie's form is a gaseous state.

These spiritual beings have served as a source of inspiration and fear in mythology. Pre-Islamic Arabs believed that they could control the elements and turn land into fertile ground.

101

Genies hold great mystery. These spiritual beings are part of the unseen elemental kingdom. They cannot shift into any form, animal, or human. It is believed that they have the power to manifest anyone's desires and to transform your life.

In popular Western culture, they are often concealed within old lamps. If the individual rubs the genie lamp, they become the master of the genie and are granted three wishes.

The Three Wishes

What would you wish for? The Aladdin genie set some ground rules around the wishes. Aladdin could not:

- receive more than three wishes.
- kill anyone.
- have anyone fall in love.
- bring anyone back from the dead.

Do you believe there is a price to pay for receiving a wish or blessing? Some individuals believe that there must be balance in the world. When you step back and take the time to really consider the concept of "wishes", you may find that it comes with some downsides.

1. If you spend all of your time wishing in life, are you missing out on being present in the moment?
2. If you receive a wish, did you consider the highest and best outcome for all OR did you wish for your own personal gain?
3. Is there cause-and-effect outcomes from wishing?

ARE YOU A GENIE?

Take some time and think about these questions:

1. Do you seek independence and freedom in all areas of your life?
2. Do you hate small or confined spaces?
3. Do you love shiny objects?
4. Do you like to create magical moments for the people that you love and care about?
5. Do you find that you overcommit your time and energy?
6. Do you gravitate towards art, fine foods, and travel?
7. Do you love fine jewelry?
8. Do you enjoy being the life of the party OR tend to avoid parties?
9. Do you tend to have a practical perspective towards most things in your life?
10. Do you get frustrated with other individuals who do not seem to ever be satisfied with their life?
11. Are you a people pleaser in most areas of your life?
12. Do you secretly do special things for other individuals without taking credit for your actions?
13. Do you resist the societal push to have material things?

How many of these did you answer yes? _____

Do you think that you are a genie?

LESSONS LEARNED

Genies have observed the outcome of human greed. Some individuals will never be satisfied with their life. They continue to compete with their co-workers, family, and friends in their lives. There is a real lesson in being grateful for who you are and what you have earned in your life.

An individual with a genie soul may be:
- creating magical moments and celebrations for loved ones.
- pushing away riches and gold.
- requiring space in their home and workspace.
- striving for a simpler life filled with joy and happiness.
- wanting independence and freedom in all areas of purpose.

They will need to be aware of these pitfalls:
- allowing too many restrictions on their life.
- burning up all their energies by helping others.
- having others take advantage of their kindness & generosity.
- limiting themselves by feeling unworthy of success.
- overcommitting to tasks and projects.

ENERGY OF MAY

The month of **May** holds the energy of **Creativity**. This is the month to get creative as you step out of Spring and into the Summer months. Spring brings the opportunity to plant new seeds and to create new things in our lives. Take time to get creative, so that you can manifest new things in your life.

CREATIVITY

As we move into the energies of Creativity, you are being asked to connect with your creative juices to create new things in your life.

Ask yourself these questions:

- What has gotten stagnant in my life?
- Where am I stuck?
- What would I like to create?
- What are some new seeds that I could plant with the universe?

The month of May brings in a few celebrations including Mother's Day and Memorial Day. It is a time to remember the people that are connected to this national recognized holidays. We are moving toward summer. The children are getting excited about the end of school. The energy and excitement is moving into our spaces and many plan summer vacations and getaways.

Spring has allowed us to plant new seeds of intention for our lives. This is an opportunity to be creative and play. Here are some ideas to consider:

- Find a way to play, laugh, and dance by gathering friends or family. This is a great time for a family reunion, picnic, or a family outing.
- Schedule a playdate with a friend or family member.
- Take a class on painting, ceramics, pottery, woodwork, etc.
- Check out our Magical Fairy Playshops on Mother's Day weekend.

SACRED PATHWAY

MEMBERSHIP
Online Education & Resources

SACRED PATHWAY LINK

Do you love these programs? Did you know that you can have access to all of them online with our **Sacred Pathway Membership**?

✨ **Sacred Pathway Membership** ✨
Your gateway to spiritual growth, sacred wisdom, and everyday magic.

Step into Sacred Pathway—an inspiring online community designed to nurture your soul, expand your knowledge, and deepen your spiritual practice. Whether you're just beginning your journey or have been walking your path for years, Sacred Pathway offers a treasure trove of resources you can explore anytime, anywhere.

With your membership, you'll enjoy full access to beautifully curated Resource Libraries filled with guided meditations, crystal wisdom, herbal magic, essential oil guides, spirit animal insights, and so much more. You'll also discover educational programs on cleansing rituals, creating sacred space, connecting with angels and archangels, crystal alchemy, and other transformative spiritual teachings.

At just **$22 a month**, Sacred Pathway gives you the freedom to connect and learn on your own schedule, while still feeling part of a like-minded, heart-centered community.

Your spiritual journey is unique. Let Sacred Pathway be the lantern that lights the way. 🌟

Find out more at:

https://discoveryourspiritualgifts.academy/sacred-pathways

SACRED PATHWAY PAGE

✨ *Did You Know We Have Four Magical Websites?* ✨

Each website is filled with resources, articles, classes, and inspiration to support your spiritual journey. Here's a quick guide to help you explore all the sacred spaces we offer:

✨ Discover Your Spiritual Gifts ✨

www.discoveryourspiritualgifts.com

This is our heart center—focused on community, connection, and spiritual growth. DYSG is home to an average of 30 professional practitioners offering sessions, classes, and special events. Visit our monthly calendar pages to see what's happening and join in the magic.

FREE Gift:

When you subscribe to our weekly newsletter (sent every Friday), you'll receive a free ebook as a thank-you for joining our community.

SCAN CODE

✨ Sacred Temple Mystery School ✨
www.sacredtemplemysteryschool.com

This site is for the seeker of deeper wisdom. Our mystery school programs are immersive, transformative, and designed for those ready to commit to their spiritual path. You'll find an abundance of teachings, Wheel of the Year resources, monthly energy updates, and Tarot guidance.

FREE Gift:

Receive the ebook "What Priest or Priestess Archetype Are You?" when you join our monthly newsletter (sent on the 2nd Monday).

✨ DYSG Online Academy ✨
www.discoveryourspiritualgifts.academy

Created for those who cannot attend in person—or who want to continue learning anytime from anywhere. Explore self-paced online classes taught by Vialet on a variety of spiritual topics.

Miss a live class? You may find it available online!
Connect with our *YouTube channel* and dive deeper into our teachings.

Sacred Pathways Membership:

A thriving online community offering classes, resource libraries, and exclusive content—only $22/month.

✨ **Vialet B Rayne** ✨

www.vialetrayne.com OR www.vialetbrayne.com

Meet Vialet, explore her offerings, and discover the rich tapestry of her spiritual studies and experience. This site is your go-to for her personal teachings, services, and wisdom.

She also hosts the **Sacred Magic Podcast**, a weekly exploration of mystical teachings and real-world spiritual insight.

You'll find Vialet's books available in the website Bookstore as well.

FREE Gift:

Receive the ebook "Seven Sacred Keys" when you join her monthly newsletter (sent on the 4th Monday).

Navigation Tip

You can easily move between all four websites by using the footer navigation buttons located at the bottom of each page.

KNOWLEDGE CHECK

#1. This program connected to these crystals:

- [ ] Tourmaline, Selenite, Sodalite and Sunstone
- [ ] Tiger Eye Gold, Red Jasper, Sunstone and Honey Calcite
- [ ] Bumble Bee Jasper, Carnelian, Orange Calcite and Sodalite
- [ ] Blue Lace Agate, Howlite, Amethyst and Larimar

#2. This program connected with these herbs:

- [ ] Marigold and Yarrow
- [ ] Chamomile and Nettle
- [ ] Red Rose and Hibiscus
- [ ] Peppermint and Orange Peel

#3. These are all ways to move energy EXCEPT:

- [ ] Open windows
- [ ] Hand a wind chime
- [ ] Relax and take a nap
- [ ] Dance to uplifting music

#4. Bumble bee jasper activates this chakra:

- [ ] Sacral Chakra
- [ ] Earth Chakra
- [ ] Earth Chakra
- [ ] Throat Chakra

KNOWLEDGE CHECK

#5. The Be Determined Ritual used this crystal:

- [ ] Selenite
- [ ] Citrine
- [ ] Black Onyx
- [ ] Red Jasper

#6. All of these are top note essential oils EXCEPT:

- [ ] Basil
- [ ] Patchouli
- [ ] Lemon
- [ ] Spearmint

#7. All of these are base note essential oils EXCEPT:

- [ ] Cedarwood
- [ ] Vanilla
- [ ] Rose
- [ ] Frankincense

#8. The Banishing An Obstacle ritual uses this crystal:

- [ ] Carnelian
- [ ] Selenite
- [ ] Bloodstone
- [ ] Red Jasper

KNOWLEDGE CHECK

#9. This moon cycle is when the moon is getting to a fuller size:

- [ ] Waxing Moon
- [ ] New Moon
- [ ] Waning Moon
- [ ] Gibbous Moon

#10. All the statements can be used to dissolve a thought or statement EXCEPT:

- [ ] Cancel, Cancel, Cancel
- [ ] Delete, delete, delete
- [ ] Erase, erase, erase
- [ ] I AM . . .